THE MUSIC MAN
Till There Was You

Words & Music by Meredith Willson

BROADWAY SHOWSTOPPERS!!!

Wise Publications
London/New York/Sydney/Cologne

Also available...
WEST END SHOWSTOPPERS!!!
Twenty all-time greats from the
biggest West End hits of recent years,
complete with lyrics and guitar chords.
Relive the great shows.

Exclusive distributors:
Music Sales Limited
8/9 Frith Street,
London W1V 5TZ,
England.

Music Sales Pty Limited
120 Rothschild Avenue,
Rosebery, NSW 2018,
Australia.

This book © Copyright 1989 by
Wise Publications
UK ISBN 0.7119.1541.5
Order No.AM71978

Designed by Pearce Marchbank Studio
Cover-photography by Julyan Hawkins
Compiled by Peter Evans

Music Sales' complete catalogue lists thousands of
titles and is free from your local music shop, or direct from
Music Sales Limited. Please send £1 in stamps for postage to
Music Sales Limited, 8/9 Frith Street, London W1V 5TZ.

Printed in the United Kingdom by
Caligraving Limited, Thetford, Norfolk.

WHERE'S CHARLEY?
Once In Love With Amy

Words & Music by Frank Loesser

Stranger In Paradise

Words & Music by Robert Wright & George Forrest

10

11

SHOW BOAT

Ol' Man River

Music by Jerome Kern
Words by Oscar Hammerstein II

Dat's de ol' stream dat I long to cross. _____

Refrain *(very slowly, with deep expression)*

Ol' man riv-er, dat ol' man riv-er, He must know sump-in', but

don't say noth-in', He jus' keeps roll-in', He keeps on roll-in' a-

long. _____ He don't plant 'ta-ters, he

Can't Help Lovin' Dat Man

Music by Jerome Kern
Words by Oscar Hammerstein II

De an - gels done plan. _____

De chimb-ley's smok-in', De roof is leak-in' in, _____ But he don't _____

_____ seem to care, He can be hap-py Wid jus' a sip of

gin. _____

I ev - en loves him when _____

back dat day is fine, ___ De sun will shine.

He can come home ___ as late as can be, ___ Home wid-out him ___ ain't

no home to me, ___ Can't help lov - in' dat man ___ of

mine.

mine. ___

ANNIE

Tomorrow

Music by Charles Strouse
Words by Martin Charnin

SWEET CHARITY
Big Spender

Words by Dorothy Fields
Music by Cy Coleman

I don't pop my cork for ev - 'ry guy I see.___

Hey! Big Spend-er,___ Spend a lit - tle time___ with

me. Would-n't you like to have

fun, fun, fun? How's a-bout a few laughs laughs? I can show you a

If My Friends Could See Me Now

Words by Dorothy Fields
Music by Cy Coleman

And I Am Telling You I'm Not Going

Music by Henry Krieger
Lyrics by Tom Eyen

SOUTH PACIFIC
Younger Than Springtime

Words by Oscar Hammerstein II
Music by Richard Rodgers

An- gel and lov- er, heav- en and earth are you to me. And when your youth and joy in- vade my arms And fill my heart as now they do... then... Young- er than Spring- time am I, Gay- er than laugh- ter am I, An- gel and lov- er, heav- en and earth am I with you! you!

Being Alive

Music & Lyrics by Stephen Sondheim

WEST SIDE STORY
Somewhere

Music by Leonard Bernstein
Lyrics by Stephen Sondheim

There's a time for us, Some-day a time for us.

Time to-geth-er with time to spare, Time to learn, time to care.

Some-day, ___ some-where ___ We'll find a new way of liv-ing, ___

We'll find a way of for-giv-ing, ___ some-where. ___

THE MUSIC MAN
Seventy Six Trombones

Words & Music by Meredith Willson

Eb7   Bb7   Eb7   G7

buh ___ buh buh buh buh buh buh. ___

C   Ebdim   G7   C#dim G7

Sev - en - ty Six Trom - bones hit the coun - ter - point, ___

C

___ While a hun - dred and ten cor - nets played the air. ___

C7   F

___ Then I mod - est - ly took my place as the one and on - ly

54

bass, And I oom - pahed, oom - pahed, oom - pah - pahed,

oom - pahed up and down the square. Sev - en - ty

square.

Smoke Gets In Your Eyes

Music by Jerome Kern
Words by Otto Harbach

THE MOST HAPPY FELLA
Standing On The Corner

Words & Music by Frank Loesser

D.S. al Fine 𝄋

I'm the cat that got the cream, Have-n't got a girl,—
Sat-ur-day and I'm so broke, Could-n't buy a girl,—

But I can dream, Have-n't got a girl,—
a nick-el coke, Still I'm liv-ing like—

But I can wish, so I take me down to Main Street And
A mil-lion-aire, when I take me down to Main Street And

that's where I se-lect my i-mag-i-na-ry dish!
I re-view the ha-rem pa-rad-ing for me there.

D.S. al Fine

The Most Happy Fella

Words & Music by Frank Loesser

spring-time fast! **F** **C#7** She's-a make the green come

on ___ the vine! **F#** **B** **Eb7** **Ab** She's-a send me ___ her

G pho - to - graph **Am7** And she was ask - in' - a me ___ for **D6/7**

G mine. *(With great vigor)* I'm The Most Hap - py Fel - la

f (ben marcato)

HOW TO SUCCEED IN BUSINESS
WITHOUT REALLY TRYING
I Believe In You

Words & Music by Frank Loesser

Briskly with Confidence

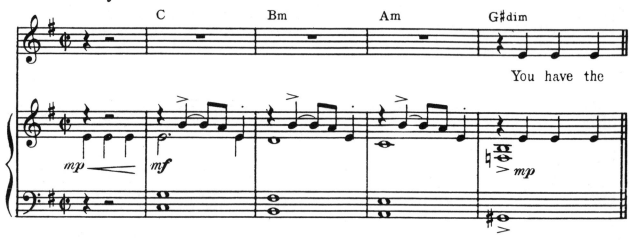

You have the

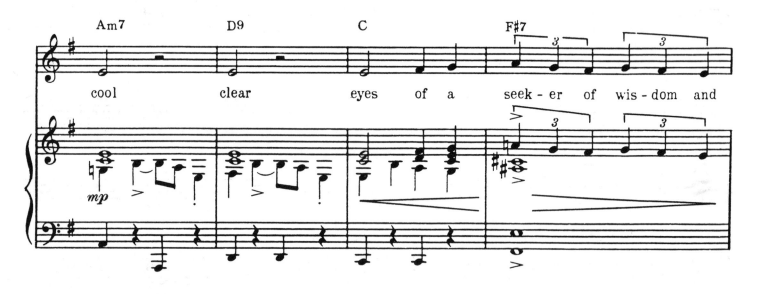

cool clear eyes of a seek - er of wis - dom and

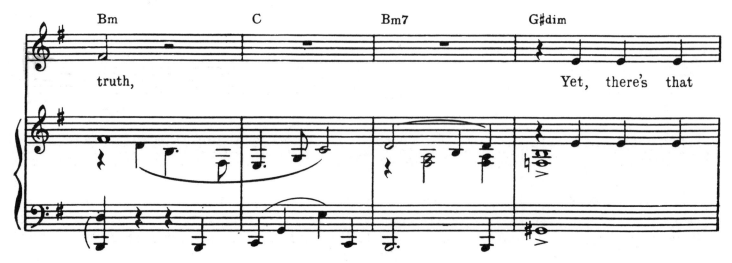

truth,   Yet, there's that

feel your hand grasp-ing mine _____ and I take heart, _____ I take heart. To see the cool clear eyes of a seek-er of wis-dom and truth, Yet there's that slam

My Darling, My Darling

Words & Music by Frank Loesser

I've Told Ev'ry Little Star

Music by Jerome Kern
Words by Oscar Hammerstein II

I make up things to say on my way to you,

On my way to you, I find things to say.

sigh_____ Oh, dear.

Refrain (gracefully)

I've told ev-'ry lit-tle star, Just how sweet I think you are, Why have-n't I told you?

I've told rip-ples in a brook,

Made my heart an o-pen book, Why have-n't I told you?_____ Friends ask me: Am I in love? I al-ways an-swer "Yes," Might as well con-fess, If I don't, they guess.

May - be you may know it too, Oh, my dar - ling, if you do, Why have - n't you told me?_